THE GREETER'S MANUAL

THE GREETER'S MANUAL

A Guide
for
Warm-Hearted
Churches

LESLIE PARROTT

ZondervanPublishingHouse
Grand Rapids, Michigan

A Division of HarperCollins*Publishers*

THE GREETER'S MANUAL
COPYRIGHT © 1993 BY LESLIE PARROTT

Published by Zondervan Publishing House
5300 Patterson Avenue, SE, Grand Rapids, Michigan 49530

Parrott, Leslie, 1922–
  The Greeter's Manual: A guide for Warm-hearted Churches /
  Leslie Parrott.
    p. cm.
  ISBN 0-310-37481-2
  1. Church greeters I. Title.
  BV705.P29 1993
  253'.7–dc20
                      93-1463
                       CIP

Cover design by Cindy Davis

Printed in the United States of America

00 01 02 03 04 05 / DP / 15 14 13 12 11 10

To two of the best church greeters I ever knew,
Chet and Bernita Hill,
who helped make the foyer of their church
a place of organized friendliness
and mutual acceptance

CONTENTS

Preface

HOW TO USE
THIS MANUAL

Back when ushering was still a stepchild in many churches, the idea of an official group of warm-hearted church greeters had not even been conceived—certainly not born. In earlier days, the local congregation focused on the basic ministries that met the needs of churches in an agrarian society. In those days, churches were primarily interested in preaching, home visitation, and care of the sick. Church greeting, as an official member of the church family of lay services, was a long time coming.

HOW GREETERS CAME TO BE

In that former era, the parson (old English for the "person") was a lone figure in the community who had no staff of either lay or ordained people to extend or specialize the ministry of the church. There were no Christian education wings on church buildings; fellowship halls were nonexistent. Laypeople attended services, paid their tithes, and were ministered to by the preacher. Except for raising an occasional barn, most good works were private.

Most congregations began their family of lay ministries with the birth of a Sunday school. The idea of a teacher in the church was conceived, and, in due time, the eldest child in the family of Christian volunteers was born. The model for the Sunday school was the one-room public school. Patterned after the pastor, the Sunday school teacher was an authority figure who stood up front and lectured the pupils, children or adults, as though they were sitting in a church service.

Soon after the need for a Sunday school had been generally accepted in local churches came the idea of "special" music beyond the accustomed congregational singing. Music by choirs, small groups, and soloists was rapidly taken to heart as an important ministry for lay volunteers. Except for the more sophisticated city churches, ushers, during this early era of developing lay church ministries, were primarily offering takers. In many churches ushers functioned part-time, sitting with their wives in their customary pews, offering plate in hand, waiting for the pastor to "call" them into service. With the offering taken, the ushers returned to their empty places in the pews, satisfied that their service had been rendered.

In those early days, there were no God-called youth ministers in the modern sense of the idea, except for a specialized group of young evangelists gifted in converting teens to Christ and the church. Young married couples in the congregation supported each other and fulfilled their parenting responsibilities the best way they could. Raising children was strictly a family concern and not a responsibility of the church. And senior citizens had not yet been discovered as the VIPs they have come to be.

The family of lay volunteers in evangelical churches expanded noticeably about the time churches started focusing on these differentiated needs among people in the congregation. Pastors and congregations began realizing their single-barreled shotgun approach did not hit the needs of all church members evenly. Ideas for better quality and more specific Christian service to all age groups and interest groups within the church spawned the age of trained volunteers and the rise of a professional staff in the church to serve as teachers and ministers for specific groups such as children, youth, senior citizens, and graded choirs.

Later, ushers were among these church workers who were recognized as important, who needed to be recruited carefully and trained adequately for the much-needed service they were to render.

And now the time has come when most churches recognize the need to recruit, organize, train, and motivate a cadre of the right kinds of people to officially represent the pastor. The greeter is the vehicle through which the church board and congregation can provide to its own people, and especially to newcomers, a personal expression of Christian warmth and welcome. Greeting is now a ministry all its own. And, among the warmest and most friendly congregations, this ministry of the church greeter extends beyond the foyer. It begins in the parking lot.

THE IMPORTANCE OF THE CUSTOMER

The birth of greeters as an official organization for Christian service was probably urged along by the national and international attention shift in business philosophy from what had been a single focus on the product to a concern for the customer who is the potential buyer and user of the product.

Important books and studies by nationally recognized authorities have stimulated this new focus on the customer. These include:

1. *Marketing for Non-Profit Organizations*, by Philip Kotler of Northwestern University. Kotler has brought the customer concept into the classroom, even into some seminaries. One of his major chapters is "The Responsive Organization: Meeting Customer Needs."
2. *In Search of Excellence*, by Tom Peters and Robert Waterman. Written a decade ago, their influential study included such chapters as "Close to the Customer" and "Hands-on, Value Driven."
3. Peter Drucker, probably the most prestigious authority and writer on business affairs since World War II, recently made a sudden shift in his work to give his time and energy for the rest of his life to the study of nonprofit organizations, including the church. In his monumental series of training tapes (Vol. 1) Drucker says, "The church must look on the outside for an opportunity of need which can be met on the inside. The church is people driven and must be highly sensitized to their needs."
4. *Learned Optimism*, by Martin Seligman. One of the latest books that focuses on customers and those who work with them. If he were a pastor—and he is not—I am sure

Seligman would put his best people on the front line in the foyer to welcome the folks and to create the warm atmosphere which is basic in serving the needs of a congregation.

ORGANIZED FRIENDLINESS

It is difficult to exaggerate the importance of the ministry of church greeters. In earlier times, the pastor used his access to the pulpit to urge people toward greater friendliness in the church. But the ideal of a friendly congregation did not include the thought of organized church greeters in the foyer. If there was an attempt at church door friendliness, the pastor, who was sometimes joined at the church door by his wife, was it. But even in this instance, the pastor's expression of friendliness was given to the people as they *left* the sanctuary, not as they arrived.

Today, however, organized friendliness that focuses on the needs of the people from the time they enter the parking lot until they sit in the pew, is made effective by an official group of people who have the gifts and graces to express social warmth and are willing to commit their time and energy to this ministry.

Like other kinds of Christian service, the importance of greeters in the foyer has steadily increased, and their work has been institutionalized into a regular lay ministry of the church. The head greeter is chosen with the same care once invested in the choosing of a Sunday school superintendent. And the result of the work of greeters, when done well, is a plus factor in the total ministry of the church. Every church can, and must, have an effective group of official greeters.

Church greeters need to be carefully recruited, well-organized, adequately trained, and fully motivated. An honest smile and a heartfelt handshake may be a cup of cold water given in Christ's name to a thirsty soul. This greeter's manual is intended to be a guide for these purposes.

George Burns once told an acting class that the most important quality in an actor is sincerity. "And, if you can fake sincerity, you've got it made." The fact is, you can't. Affected sincerity is as phony as a three dollar bill, but when kindness and friendliness are sincere, greeting becomes a ministry.

FILLING THE NEED

This manual is written to fill three specific needs in churches who take their warm-hearted ministry of church greeters seriously:

- The need for motivation

Many churches need more appreciation for the importance of a church greeters' ministry. Far too many congregations expect a warm spirit of Christian friendliness to inhabit the foyer of the church without any strategy to make it happen. When the pastor begins to understand the importance of church greeting and clarifies it as a priority, then the greeters themselves will move toward a standard of excellence which will lift their work to the level of ministry.

- The need for a ready reference tool

Taken as a whole, this manual can be a helpful tool for improving the quality of greeting in your church. However, each greeter also needs a copy of *The Greeter's Manual* for his or her own purposes. Work out individual problems according to the code of common sense needed in your local situation. Just as no two congregations are alike, no two greeters are the same. Therefore, some suggestions in this manual may miss the mark for specific persons in certain situations. Everything is comparable. Oscar Wilde, who was raised in California near the blue Pacific Ocean, saw the Atlantic for the first time and said it was disappointing. It did not compare well with what he knew about oceans. Avoid the consequences of rigidity. Do not *adopt* this manual blindly, but use common sense in *adapting* its ideas and guidelines to your church and to your assignment as a church greeter.

- The need for training classes

The Greeter's Manual is designed for use as a teaching text in local churches. It can serve as a study guide for training classes where ideas are discussed and local strategies and procedures are developed. It needs to be read in private and studied by underlining important thoughts. The content and application of the material can be expanded by using the questions for discussion which are included at the end of each chapter.

As the writer of this greeter's manual, my prayer is that you and your church will enjoy a more effective ministry with your church greeting because you have taken time to study the helps and guides which follow in the next five chapters.

1

THE MINISTRY
OF CHURCH GREETERS

Churches regularly sustain the same hierarchy in Sunday
morning ministries. It is not planned that way; it just is. Some
things that happen in church on Sunday morning are high on
people's priority list while others are not. What some people
contribute to a worship service is recognized by the congregation as more valuable to Christian nurturing than what others
do. Worship is like the Bible; it may all be inspired but it is not
all of equal value. The following hierarchy of Sunday morning
ministries is broadly accepted.

THE HIERARCHY OF MINISTRIES

1. Preaching

If anyone's name is on the permanent church sign, it is the
man or woman who usually occupies the Sunday morning
pulpit. It is not uncommon for the name of the person
preaching the sermon to appear in bold type in the church
bulletin. People may even express disappointment when they
arrive at church to learn the regular preaching minister is absent
and someone else is in the pulpit.

While Dr. Calliandro was still serving as Assistant Minister
to Dr. Peale at Marble Collegiate Church in New York, I arrived
for the service to be greeted on the front steps by Dr.
Calliandro, who was also talking seriously with the head
greeter. I overheard the usher say to Dr. Calliandro, "I feel
sorry for you." Moments later I learned that Dr. Peale was

home in bed, sick with the flu, and the Assistant Pastor was to preach in his place. Like everybody else, I was disappointed, but unlike everybody else, I considered leaving. After the service, I was glad I had stayed, for Dr. Calliandro preached a good sermon ending with a life-absorbing story which I have remembered even after all these years.

Paul, who wrote about the "foolishness of preaching," also wrote, "How can they call on the one they have not believed in? And, how can they believe in the one of whom they have not heard? And how can they hear without someone preaching to them?" (Rom. 10:14). Most of us will agree with Paul on the paradox of preaching, and agree with the church-going public that preaching is the first priority on the Sunday morning worship agenda.

2. Teaching

Next to preaching, Martin Luther believed teaching was the highest calling of God. Teaching is mentioned scores of times in the New Testament. Jesus was called Teacher and often taught outdoors in both Galilee and Judea. Teaching is listed among the spiritual gifts. On his missionary journeys, Paul went first to the synagogues where he taught from the Scriptures. It is fully Christian and biblical that great numbers of people in churches everywhere are committed to teaching, a ministry that approximates the importance of preaching in the hierarchy of Sunday morning ministries.

The pastor who preaches without teaching, or the church that evangelizes without nurturing the converts is obscuring the full purpose of the cross and is missing one of the vital ministries of the Holy Spirit: "But the Counselor, the Holy Spirit, whom the Father will send in my name, will teach you all things and . . . will guide you into all truth" (John 14:26; 16:13).

3. Celebration of music to the glory of God

I can remember an era in the church where I attended when music consistently rivaled the impact of preaching and teaching in Sunday worship. The just-right combination of a superb organist, a polished professional pianist, and a nationally known minister of music who directed a carefully recruited choir, had brought the ministry of our church music to an inspiring level. There were mornings when the singing lifted the people to a worship plateau usually reserved for the pastor's sermon. The music consistently fulfilled the admonition of St. Paul, "Let the word of Christ dwell in you richly. . . as you sing psalms, hymns, and spiritual songs with gratitude in your hearts to God" (Col. 3:16).

However, whether or not the music electrifies the worship atmosphere is not the point. Churchgoing people love music. And a church with inspiring music is likely to have a larger congregation for the sermon than one without it.

4. Organized friendliness of ushers and greeters, especially greeters

The Sunday ministry of church greeters is a late bloomer in the family of volunteer Christian services. It is an adjunct to preaching, teaching, and music. But it is a ministry, a very important one, and becoming more so. The sinner and the saint understand the language of kindness equally well. When someone is emotionally down, an ounce of kindness is worth a pound of preaching. This is one of the reasons why church greeters have an important ministry. Anyone can pass out bulletins. But Christian kindness is a ministry for church greeters who care deeply about people.

THE BIBLICAL PRECEDENT

All churches need to rise to the occasion as modern day counterparts to the ancient doorkeepers in the house of the Lord. Congregations without an organized church greeters' ministry need to create one. Others need to improve the ministry already in place. This is especially true in smaller and mid-sized congregations which have lagged behind their more aggressive counterparts in larger churches. And all churches, large and small, need to celebrate organized friendship with the Psalmist who wrote, "How lovely is your dwelling place, O LORD Almighty! . . .I would rather be a doorkeeper in the house of my God than dwell in the tents of the wicked" (Ps. 84:1, 10).

The Biblical reminder of the importance of a doorkeeper ministry comes from an ancient family chronicle. The spirit of family pride comes through the story of Shallum, who was a

member of the fourth generation among "the fellow gatekeep-
ers from his family responsible for guarding the thresholds of
the Tent just as their fathers had been responsible for guarding
the entrance to the dwelling of the LORD" (1 Chron. 9:19).
Serving as a doorkeeper in the house of the Lord was no small
matter in those days. Nor is it now.

From the tabernacle to the temple to the synagogue to the
New Testament church, the ministry of greeting has taken on
increasing importance. For more than 300 years Christians
worshiped mainly in homes or house churches. Therefore the
host actually welcomed the Sunday morning worshipers into
his own home.

In Rome, where Christians were afraid to gather openly in
homes, they appropriated the Catacombs—an interlinked
system of tunnels beneath the city—for their places of worship.
It takes little imagination to visualize the personal warmth and
the authentic welcome extended to each other as one isolated
Christian after another slipped past the guards to join the
underground believers for worship.

Friendship is at the very heart of Christian brotherhood. It
has been there from the beginning. All the modern church has
added to the important atmosphere of mutual acceptance in the
New Testament church is the identification of volunteer
greeters as an organized group. Thankfully, the work of
greeters in the modern day church has been organized and
institutionalized as a recognized ministry in the family of
Christian volunteers. Their much needed gifts and graces have
been honed by adequate training and experience to raise their
level of effectiveness, and the church foyer has been designated
as their place of service. In warm-hearted churches everywhere,
official church greeters have become a recognized ministry
based on a biblical precedent.

THE ONE-ANOTHER MINISTRY

No assignment in the church is more one-on-one than the
ministry of church greeters. The foyer is their chapel, the
information desk their pulpit, and the walk-around spaces their
parish.

In contrast to the greeters at the doors of the church,
pastors welcome the congregation en masse from behind a self-

protecting pulpit. As some note, pastors stand several steps above contradiction, while they literally look down on the people. Teachers welcome classes in the isolation of small rooms behind closed doors. Choir members wear robes intended to obscure individual personalities and blend a large number of persons into a single unit as they sing their call to worship. Some choirs do not even look at the people as they sing their choral welcome, but keep their eyes on the director. But church greeters have a one-another ministry, face to face, hand to hand, heart to heart with the people they are called to serve. Church greeters in large churches may minister in multiple parking lots or in large foyers, but their Christian service is to one customer at a time just like it is in the smallest church. And to make their work even more important, church greeters are the first people others meet when arriving at church.

On Main Street, out where people make their daily bread, there has lately arisen a sudden and intense interest concerning first impressions made on customers as they enter a place of business. On a bank board where I served, the directors often expressed their concern that tellers, who are the first line of encounter with customers, are at the bottom of the bank's totem pole in salaries and status. In our bank, the best paid people worked with secretaries behind closed doors in order to guard their offices against random access and thus conserve the banker's time and energy for important matters. But down on the main floor where customers came and went, the ambassadors of goodwill were people serving at entry level jobs.

I have often wondered if the perceptions of church greeters in some congregations are not also confused. Are people who do not sing in the choir, teach classes, or usher, chosen to serve as church greeters because they lack talents in those other areas? I hope not! Low esteem, little reward, and almost no recognition have often been the lot of church greeters who serve on the front line. In churches where this attitude prevails, it is time for change.

If Paul were alive today, he would have something to say to church greeters. It would be the same message he gave to Christians serving a remote assignment in Colosse. "Whatever you do, work at it with all your heart, . . . It is the Lord Christ you are serving" (Col. 3:23, 24).

Church greeting must be elevated to its full status as a one-another ministry. What people will not do for money, they will do free of charge and with great loyalty if they are accorded recognition and can feel a sense of ministry in their assignment.

In Paul's letter to the Romans, he refers to the one-another ministry seven times. Each of these admonitions works together with all the others to create a spiritual and biblical base for the ministry of church greeters.

Accept one another

"Accept one another . . . as Christ accepted you" (Rom. 15:7). This is the ministry of mutual acceptance. It rests on Christ's teaching of unconditional love which is free from color bias, racial prejudice, and inordinate concern for status.

A verbal greeting and the offer of a handshake is a way of focusing on the other person. These words and gestures say, "You are somebody. You matter to me. We are glad you are here. I want you to feel welcome."

On the other hand, the church greeter who has difficulty shifting the focus from within himself or herself outward to the other person is falling short. The important question is not "How am I doing?" or "How do I look?" but "How are they doing?" and "How do they feel?"

The choir welcomes people from the elevated choir loft. The pastor welcomes people from behind the pulpit. The teacher welcomes pupils from within the classroom. But it is the business of church greeters to receive people upon their immediate arrival at church. It is the church greeter who is out there on the firing line, dealing with people firsthand in a one-on-one setting without the advantage of intervening buffers. The church greeter absorbs whatever attitudes and stored-up feelings the worshiper has brought to church. Therefore, the welcome from the greeter may be happily received or, on occasion, he or she may be called on to absorb the negative effects of someone's unresolved stress. Unfortunately, for some people, too much happiness too early in the morning just brings out their worst side.

However, the effective church greeter never shows signs of recoiling from a negative barb, a slight incivility, or even a harsh word from some harried worshiper who is more occupied with their own thoughts than with the need to respond to a greeting. Greeters: ignore the problems but receive the people. As Christ has received us with unconditional love, accept each and every person who comes through your church door just as they are, warts and all.

Honor one another

"Honor one another" (Rom. 12:10). This is the one-another ministry of an encouraging word. One of the skills developed by the most effective kinds of church greeters is the capacity to come up with a few words, even a one-liner, that enhances someone's moment of entry through the church door.

This need to recognize other people with a word that attaches to their purpose is important. Since most families arrive about the same time each Sunday and enter through the same door, it is good for the church greeter to be sensitive to them as people with whom they have an ongoing relationship of sorts. It does not take much concentration to be aware of the achievements, concerns, and hopes among the regulars you face each Sunday. Any inquiry into the well-being of a married child in another town, a concern for the crops to be harvested, the physical improvement of an ill family member, the passing of a child to the next grade, is the raw material from which words of encouragement come.

Be kind to one another

"Be devoted to one another" (Rom. 12:10). This is the one-another ministry of kindness. Acts of kindness are the sweet-smelling essence of a heavenly aroma. Nothing perfumes the air like an act of kindness.

Many people come to church on Sunday weary from a week of frustration. They need to be uplifted. They have not come to church for an additional burden but to receive help in carrying the one they already have. Their self-image may already have been assaulted with more than their fair share of rejection and self-doubt. What they need to experience is a greeter with an understanding heart. It is the church greeter who opens the door to a kindly church, to the ministry of a helpful pastor, and to the potential of a spiritually refreshing worship experience. High in the priorities of the human heart is the need for acceptance. The human race lives with an insatiable desire for the milk of human kindness. It is not a parking lot greeter's place to rebuke drivers for failing to stay within the lines; he or she is there to minister through kindness. It is impossible for a church greeter to fake a smile and be believed if his or her body language sends a rebuke to the entering worshiper. Kindness, kindness, kindness: These are three basic qualities of a church greeter.

Love one another

"Love one another" (Rom. 13:8). This is the one-another ministry of unconditional goodwill. This is the fulfilling ministry: "For he who loves his fellow man has fulfilled the law" (Rom. 13:8). This kind of love is expressed in a positive attitude toward people in general. It is a love which excludes verbal abuse from any and all communications. It is an attitude of love toward life in general and people in particular.

In the ancient world where Paul lived, there were three common kinds of love spoken of by people on the streets of Greek and Roman cities: (1) Sometimes people used the word "love" to express the intense concern of a man for a woman. This is sexual love; (2) Other times people used the word "love" to talk about the strong bond among people who are legally connected through birth or marriage. This is family love, and quite different from sexual love; (3) And finally, people in the ancient world sometimes used the word "love" to express the mutual bond of respect and appreciation people have for each other, just because they like one another. This is love for a friend.

To these three kinds of love—sexual, family, and friendship—Jesus added another, agape. This unconditional love is expressed in abounding goodwill toward people who may or may not have earned it, and may or may not accept it. This is love without prior conditions. It is unconditional. Agape love makes it possible for Christians to "owe no man anything but to love one another." The church greeter who can love all the people unconditionally renders a high level of Christian service at the church door.

Understand one another

"Stop passing judgment on one another" (Rom. 14:13). This is Paul's only negative one-another statement. However, a judgmental attitude can only be overcome by a spirit of understanding. The change from a judgmental to an understanding mind requires a personal decision and self-discipline empowered by the Holy Spirit. In the full statement of this one-another admonition, Paul said, "Therefore, let us stop passing judgment on one another. Instead, make up your mind not to put any stumbling block or obstacle in your brother's way."

The church greeter also has a responsibility to measure up to life's moral twin peaks of integrity and purity. It is most unfortunate for a church greeter on Sunday morning to be confronted at the door of the church by someone who has known him or her in a compromising situation. It is the church greeter's business to be nonjudgmental toward all who come through the door of the church. But it is even more the business of the church greeter to be sure his or her life is not a stumbling block to others, particularly to someone in the fellowship of the congregation.

Instruct one another

"Instruct one another" (Rom. 15:14). The best church greeters are role models in the Christian graces. Church greeters are pilgrims, not proclaimers. They teach by being, doing, and demonstrating, not by telling, admonishing, and finger pointing.

It is not the business of the church greeter to instruct people in the usual meaning of the word "instruct." But it is very much the business of the church greeter to be secure in himself or herself, to come across as a Christian who is living confidently in the faith which fortifies people. Church greeters become role models in direct proportion to the degree of Christian faith and happiness obtained in their own life. Christians are gracious to each other when they feel good about themselves.

Greet one another

"Greet one another with a holy kiss" (Rom. 16:16). This is the ministry of human touch, a gray area in social expression which needs to be understood and used carefully. The Victorian English and conservative Americans have only discovered the healing quality of the human touch in recent decades. Children will stand in line to be hugged by their teacher. Some popular lecturers in psychology have made hugging the thing to do. Hugging is the easy therapy of the day which some people have adopted as the fullest expression of personal acceptance and appreciation.

Dr. Lloyd Ogilvie tells the story of a big rancher from Montana who came to his church in Hollywood and lined up to greet the pastor at the close of the service. In a broad Montana brogue, which fit a man from the country of the big sky, he drawled, "I've come all the way from Montana to get my hug." In the sign-off segment from the Hollywood Presbyterian Church telecast, the rancher had seen Dr. Ogilvie hug some parishioners as they were leaving the church, and now this rancher had come expecting his hug. And he got it. Much discretion is needed in using human touch. The holy kiss or the hug is almost never appropriate in greeting strangers at the church door. The gesture might very well be resisted or even resented. Not all people, even those whom we know well, want to be touched beyond a handshake, nor should they be. But Paul's references to the "holy kiss" in his Corinthian correspondence are unmistakable: "All the brothers here send you greetings. Greet one another with a holy kiss" (1 Cor. 16:20). And again in his second letter to the Corinthians, he repeated his admonition: "Greet one another with a holy kiss" (2 Cor. 13:12).

For many people, the friendly hug, or the buzz on the cheek, has become a warm way of expressing affection. However, most greeters still feel the handshake is the proper Sunday morning greeting. Instead of taking Paul's admonition literally, a handshake may be the answer for a church greeter who wants to express a genuine Christian welcome in the fullest way possible, but not with a literal kiss or hug.

IN CONCLUSION

Paul has one more one-another saying which he included in his letter to the Galatians but not in his correspondence to the Romans. To those people who had great difficulty in ridding themselves of their legalistic bias in the plan of salvation, Paul wrote: "You, my brothers, were called to be free. But do not use your freedom to indulge the sinful nature; rather, serve one another in love" (Gal. 5:13). This is the one-another ministry of service, and is surely the final word to church greeters who are called to serve. Set free from the Christian legalism that often leads to spiritual pride and condescension, the church greeter is equipped to welcome people as they are and not as he or she might *wish* they were. This is the ultimate ideal in the one-another ministry of church greeters.

DISCUSSION QUESTIONS

1. What is the hierarchy of ministries in your church and how do these relate to the role and recognition of the church greeters?
2. What do you know about Shallum in the Old Testament and what does he and his family have to do with the importance of church greeters today?
3. How does the idea of a house church in the New Testament relate to the idea and ministry of church greeters?
4. Can you find ways to relate each of the one-another sayings of Paul to the ministry of church greeters in your church?
5. Can you report on some church you have known which has made an exemplary ministry out of organized Christian friendliness?

2

THE NEED FOR WARM-HEARTED GREETERS

The recent research of Daniel Yankelovich indicates that 70% of adult Americans have many acquaintances but few close friends. One must wonder if this is also true in the average congregation. Since Americans seem to feel the need for more closeness, this may be why the highest virtue among church greeters is their willingness to express human kindness. A warm-hearted church and a kind-hearted greeter go together like the pulpit and the sermon. In church work there is no warmness without kindness. Coolness is usually rudeness.

When church greeters allow their ministry to become officious by ordering people around, the good they hope to do becomes a stumbling block. Even being efficient in directing the flow of traffic is usually unproductive to relationships. Suggest, lead, guide, or do anything else that is an extension of the human smile—but don't order people. Be a warm-hearted friend, not an officer.

The one common denominator that brings everyone down to the same level of equality is the need for human kindness. This is why Peter placed kindness above godliness and just below unconditional love in his hierarchy of Christian graces: ". . . and to godliness, brotherly kindness; and to brotherly kindness, love" (2 Peter 1:7).

1. Kindness to new people who feel strange and don't know their way around

When Paul wrote about his shipwreck on the island of Malta, the first thing he mentioned was the kindness of the people to himself and the other strangers who had landed on their beach: "The islanders showed us unusual kindness. They built a fire and welcomed us all because it was raining and cold" (Acts 28:2). And the modern day strangers who come in out of the rain and cold of the weekday hassle into the sanctuary of your church will respond to that same flame that kindles human kindness.

2. Kindness to the elderly who increasingly feel alone

In one of the bonding conversations which nourished their deep friendship, Jonathan said to David as they walked through the fields, "But show me unfailing kindness like that of the LORD as long as I live . . . and do not ever cut off your kindness from my family. . ." (1 Sam. 20:14–15). As people grow older, kindness becomes increasingly important. If you want to minister to the Jonathans of this world, just let them hear that you have been kind to their family, especially their elderly.

3. Kindness to the children who are outside their comfort zone

Hosea wrote some wonderful words about kindness to Israel, whom he called a child. "When Israel was a child . . . I led them with chords of human kindness . . . I lifted the yoke from their neck and bent down to feed them" (Hos. 11:1, 4). The most loved greeter in our church was a man who had a way with children who were uncomfortable in the spaces and sounds of a large foyer and the labyrinth of church corridors where people moved to and fro and carried on loud conversations. It is important to remember that small children may be easily lost or confused. They may be overpowered with the sight of strange adults who look like hordes of giants. Or they may just be uncertain of themselves in an unfamiliar setting. This good man always bent down, or even kneeled to say a reassuring word to a child who needed him. Because he had a reputation for loving children, he was also deeply appreciated by both the children and their parents, even their grand-parents. In an era of broken homes, abuse, and loveless families, children are open more than ever to the ministry of a loving greeter. When a child needs a hug, give it to him or her.

4. Kindness to mothers with babies in their arms and toddlers at their sides

Harried young mothers may be strong enough to do all they do, but they also are amenable to acts of kindness. Making a load lighter by lifting a package, opening the door, or helping a small child up the steps is more than a social civility. It is a way of saying "we are glad you are here" and " good things are waiting for you in this church."

5. Kindness to people who show up regularly at the same time and at the same door every week

The dependable people who attend regularly may show no visible need for kindness. They may seem uninterested in your welcome greeting. But be friendly anyway, because the rewards in your ministry do not depend on reciprocation from the people you greet, but on the love of the Lord whom you serve.

6. Kindness toward the pastor and staff who sometimes need an advocate at the door

If someone feels the need to say an unkind word about your pastor or a staff member, find a way to come down on the pastor's side. The minister's load is big enough without a church greeter adding to his or her burden by reinforcing someone's negative feelings.

7. Kindness to people with special problems such as wheelchairs and crutches

People who need specialized help because of physical problems may also need extra amounts of kindness and thoughtfulness. They may even learn to enter by your door exclusively just because they need the hug or loving pat on the shoulder you can be counted on to give. It is always good to anticipate the needs of wheelchair people, those on crutches, and those who use walkers. The elderly and the disabled need more time and more space than others, and more of the kindness you can provide.

8. Kindness to people who don't seem to need it

Sometimes kindness is misunderstood. When Peter and John were called in before the court following the healing of the lame man in Acts 3, Peter began his speech to the judge by saying, "If we are being called to account today for an act of kindness shown to a cripple . . . " (Acts 4:9). In Jerusalem or wherever you live, there are people who will resist your welcome ministry even when it is extended in kindness. The unlovable drunks who wander in, the angry teenager who sulks through the door, the sullen neurotic who is out of tune with life, and even the panhandler who manipulates Christian humanitarianism for his own purposes are not immune to a kind attitude even when they do not respond favorably. We are not admonished to be kind to the people we like, but to each other, whoever the "other" may be.

DISCUSSION QUESTIONS

1. On a scale of one to ten, just how warm-hearted do you think your church is toward strangers or people who are different than themselves?
2. What are the things church greeters in your church can do to warm up the atmosphere in the foyer?
3. What should a church greeter say to someone who speaks negatively about the pastor or someone on the staff?
4. How well is the level of love in your church contributing toward saving your children and transmitting the gospel to the next generation?
5. What would you say to someone who protests something the church board has voted for and you were not for it either?

3

DEVELOPING A
USER-FRIENDLY FOYER

In Philip Kotler's text, *Marketing for Non-Profit Organizations*, he says, "A responsive church is one which makes every effort to be sensitive to the needs and wants of those who participate. People who have first hand knowledge of these kinds of churches almost always report a high level of personal satisfaction, such as 'This is the best church I have ever attended.'" (Kotler, 1982, p.33)

Other research by people such as Barna and Callahan builds on Kotler's concern for the needs of the people by confirming the high priority among all churchgoers for good relationships. One pastor with a thriving church stated that he had learned the hard way that people do not bond to the church, the denomination, or even the services. People bond to each other. This building of friendships and relationships may be ultimately fulfilled in the small groups people join, but it begins in the foyer.

People meet each other in the foyer before and after every service. If the foyer is only a means of entry and egress, its possibilities for friendliness become lost opportunities. There is a ministry in the foyer, facilitated by the church greeters and presided over by a spiritual mâitre d' called the head greeter. He or she and the co-workers make or break the foyer as a user-friendly area. This chapter identifies and explains some of the many issues and concerns about a user-friendly foyer.

1. The challenge of multiple entrances with multiple doors

Except for the small chapel or the one-room church, congregations expect churches to have multiple entrances. These many doors open the way into the church facilities from Christian education buildings, gymnasiums, office complexes, family centers, or parking lots. And at each of these doors there needs to be a qualified greeter in place, ready to extend a good welcome to everyone.

Sometimes the main entrance to a church is served by a set of double doors with hinges on opposite sides of the frame. When I enter churches with one of these multiple doors locked, and a sign that says, "Use Other Door," I cannot help but wonder what occasion would merit opening both doors. Who are they trying to keep out, or slow down? It seems as though the church should be the easiest place in the world to enter. Surely Sunday morning worship is important enough for opening all the doors to all the entrances for whomever wants to use them.

2. Some kinds of doors are better than others

If possible, install doors with lots of appeal. Heavy varnished or painted doors look as though they belong to a private club. But church doors call for lots of glass; the more the better. If possible, install solid glass doors with lots of inviting light outside and inside the entrance to help make the approach say "Welcome." Let strangers see what is going on inside the foyer. It is intimidating for the uninitiated to face a huge dark door and wonder what is on the other side.

3. From the car door to the church door

The distance from the parked car to the church door can be, for some people, the most frustrating segment in the weekly trip from home to church. Gravel that rolls underfoot is a hazard to women in thin-soled, high-heeled shoes. Watery holes in unpaved lots are an invitation to small children. And dusty gusts of wind do not reinforce the dressed-up look and affected dignity with which some people come to church.

In smaller churches, the parking area may be fairly near

the door, but is often unpaved. In larger churches, the parking lot may be paved but requires a good walk from the car to the building. In the largest churches, there may be multiple lots, some requiring families to cross a street enroute to the nearest church entrance.

Some people arrive at Sunday school or church with their Bible, a load of books or a box of materials, or refreshments that may be needed in a class. Others, or even the same people, may arrive with one or more small children who need to be carried or guided through the parking lot to the church door.

No two churches use the same approach in meeting the needs of people arriving in the family automobile. Some churches have protective marquees so that the driver stops under the overhang to unload passengers, and then proceeds to find a parking space. A few churches offer valet parking, particularly for people with special problems.

In either case, the arriving passengers are usually greeted by someone who helps open the car door and assists the exiting passengers as needed. Some churches with large or multiple parking lots provide vans or jitneys to bring people from the parking lot to the church door. Even churches with convenient parking often station greeters strategically for opening car doors, helping people out of their cars as needed, and generally easing the way from the car to the foyer. However, some churches ignore the possibilities of a parking lot ministry with an unwritten policy that says organized friendliness begins at the church door.

4. Bulletins, greeters, and back-up greeters

Each church organizes its greeters to meet its own needs. Smaller churches may feel their needs are met by one couple or one greeter at the central entrance. Larger churches may feel that two or more couples or greeters are needed to cover the needs in their foyer while obscure doorways or secondary entrances may not need more than one couple or one greeter to welcome people.

However, the larger churches I have visited who have a significant greeter ministry, cover all entry doorways, but usually station a front line of greeters at the entrances used most often by the most people. These greeters hold bulletins in one hand and open doors with the other. They greet each person as he or she enters. Because of the traffic flow, no more than a moment can be spent with each person.

Then, behind the front line is a secondary team of greeters, deployed at an appropriate distance from the doors. They seek out persons they feel need more attention such as strangers, new attendees, or just people with special needs. These greeters usually direct the new people to the visitor table or information booth. They take enough time with new people to answer their questions and, as far as possible, make them feel at ease.

Then back of the secondary line of greeters is one or two more people who are free to be used wherever the need is. It is the job of these greeters to keep people with needs from dropping through the cracks. They also deal with special situations, often serving as a liaison with the pastor or the head usher on information which needs to be relayed to those in charge. This assignment is often handled by the head greeter.

After the service, the same greeters work their assigned zones in the foyer where they keep a ministering eye for people who are new and who need to be introduced to others. These greeters should serve during the exodus of the congregation just as they did when the people were arriving. In one particularly disappointing instance, the greeter at a back parking lot door in a very large church greeted the incoming people who had arrived for the next service, but ignored all who were leaving. The group leaving chuckled about the church which was only interested in those who were coming and not those who had already been.

5. The ultimate in greeter strategy

Churches who are not effective with their greeter ministry usually fail for one of three reasons: (1) They lack the know-how; (2) They fail to see the need; (3) They are more interested in orthodoxy than in Christian friendship. From the zero point of no organized church greeters, churches can move up the line toward the ultimate friendship strategy.

The ultimate friendship strategy includes every member of the church as a greeter. Each regular attender has his or her own private ministry of making people feel welcome. Some churches have a friendship program which calls for every member to be sensitive to all the people who are seated within an arm's length of them, and to take personal responsibility for greeting everyone within that radius. When my wife and I attended the First Baptist Church of Dallas, Texas, we felt as though all the people around us were personally glad we had come. They couldn't say enough good about their church. They almost talked us into attending their Sunday school class although we had already made another commitment.

6. Clutter, cleanliness, and creativity

The three "Cs" of concern for an attractive foyer are clutter, cleanliness, and creativity. Pastors and lay leaders who live in cluttered homes often have cluttered foyers at church. They don't see the dirt, the piles of left-over papers, the old announcements on the walls, and the lost paraphernalia strewn in the corners. To them, the foyer is not really important as a gathering place. It is just an architectural means for getting from the front door into the sanctuary. But cleanliness and orderliness are important in a user-friendly foyer.

On a boat trip in the San Juans, off the coast of Washington state, my wife and I left the dock on a Sunday morning and walked up the hill to a little white church with a Christopher Wren-type steeple. Both of us were immediately struck with the cleanliness of the foyer and the sanctuary . The windows sparkled. All the light bulbs worked. The dominant color was white. There was no clutter. Finally, my wife turned to me and said, "This place must be under the charge of a lady custodian who knows how to keep her own house spotless." In a few moments the service started, and to our amazement the pastor was a woman. If you don't have a woman pastor, maybe it would be a good idea to place the keeping of the foyer under the direction of a man or woman who has high standards when it comes to cleanliness and attractive surroundings.

The third "C" is creativity, an important word in the development of a user-friendly foyer. Seasonal decorations, signs new people need for navigating the halls of the church, a book table, placement of chairs, coat-racks, benches and other conveniences, and other such amenities make the foyer a friendly place for churchgoers to gather. Most foyers are too small, too dark, too cluttered, and too meaningless. There is lots of room for creativity in the foyer of the average church.

7. Paint, wall coverings, and lighting fixtures

The color and texture of the walls in the foyer are subtle influences on how people feel. When in doubt, use white paint. It is cheap, can be applied again as needed, and is amenable to the willing hands of volunteers. Dark wood, heavy wallpaper, and shaggy carpets have a tendency to condense spaces. Brighten up your walls. Lighten up your floor covering. Whiten your ceiling. The new feeling of airiness will be a boon to Christian sociability.

A friend of mine once borrowed money from a bank to open a small retail business. After the banker had given him the loan, he said, "I don't know about your store building on the inside, but I can tell you one thing: Double the amount of light and the customers will spend more money."

It is a fact that people tend to stay away from dark places. Darkness is intimidating. This is why doubling the amount of light in the foyers of most old churches would still not supply sufficient light. Most building committees have run out of money by the time they come to ordering the lighting, and the temptation to cut down on fixtures and wattage is too good to pass up. I have seen some adequately lit foyers but never one that had too much light. The early Christians left the catacombs many centuries ago, but architects still have a penchant for providing dark places for Christians to worship.

8. An information/reception desk

The importance of an official information center dedicated to the before and after service needs of the people, is hard to exaggerate. People need a designated place to talk with a knowledgeable person about address changes, coming events, dates and times, leaving and receiving messages, making a phone call, or expressing any concerns they may have.

When a greeter at the Washington Monument was asked for the question most often heard in her 20 years on the job, she said it was "Where is the restroom?" It would not take long to make a list of the questions asked most often in the church foyer. And it would not take much longer to provide a ready list of answers and services.

9. Greeter alertness

There are some things a greeter can't be taught and a reception desk person cannot be trained to do. Many things happen in the foyer that are not on the schedule. Mental alertness and human sensitivity are two precious possessions someone in the foyer needs on a regular basis. When to give in, when to resist, when to give out certain information, and presence of mind in an emergency are only learned by observation and experience. The pastor's secretary need not be asked to work in the reception center on Sundays, but someone of that caliber needs to be available in the foyer of most churches.

10. Pros and cons on name tags

Some churches use name tags for visitors. Other churches use name tags for everyone including the pastor. And most churches do not use name tags at all. However, name tags are most useful as a means to friendship when they are worn by everyone. Even folks who see each other in church often may not always be sure of names.

On the down side, some people resist the wearing of a name tag on their dress or suit, or feel no need for it since "I go to this church every Sunday, and everyone knows me." If a name tag program is begun, it needs to be thought through with plenty of sign-up space and ample personnel assigned to make the system work. With the use of computers, pages of peel-off alphabetized names can be prepared a month at a time and used individually as needed. I know one church who uses this system to determine the attendance record of its constituency. They have used the system for several years and are convinced of its reliability.

11. A place for coats and hats

In places where people are likely to wear coats and hats for any significant period of the year, places for hanging them are important. While I was a graduate student at Michigan State University, one thing I enjoyed, and a service I admired, was their system for checking coats, hats, and boots in the Student Center. And this was done for students. Not many churches have a vision for this kind of service to their people. But in the most user-friendly foyers, there is ample space for safekeeping of coats during church services.

12. The importance of floor coverings

Good looking, serviceable floor coverings add warmth and beauty to a user-friendly foyer. Linoleum is the cheapest covering to buy, but is likely to show wear before the church board is ready to replace it.

Contrasting black and white squares of vinyl almost always look stylish and clean cut. But these squares require a cleaning regimen that can become a problem unless the church has a willing number of volunteers or paid custodians. But when black and white floors are spotless they are impressive, if not dramatic. And, if the situation calls for it, these floors will distract people from looking up at a low or unsightly ceiling.

Wall-to-wall carpeting can be handsome, although most churches are slow to spend the amount of money necessary for top quality carpeting which can absorb the beating a foyer takes on a weekly basis. The floor covering decision is finally a matter of local choice, although consultation with a knowledgeable person who has nothing to sell may be a very good investment of time and energy.

13. Bulletin boards

Every foyer needs an ample supply of bulletin boards, well-arranged and kept up to date. A bulletin board for the pastors and staff is essential. It needs to be ample in size, well-lighted, and continuously updated. Messages and posters increasingly lose some of their effectiveness each successive week they are left unchanged. Some large organizations within the church may want their own bulletin board, which is usually a good idea as long as it too is updated weekly and the displays are attractive. Teen bulletin boards are well-received in churches with lots of young people.

14. The sanctified book table

Although some conservative people are uncomfortable with the idea of selling books because of money changing hands on Sunday, a well-kept book table under the authority of a dependable person can add much to the growth of learning and ministry in the church.

There is no such thing as a learning congregation without the pervasive habit of reading. And one of the best ways to encourage reading in a congregation is to provide the people with available books week by week. In most churches, it is better to dedicate the profits from book sales to some worthy cause in the church than to offer bargains to the purchasers. The success of this book table venture will depend entirely on the person who is chosen to be in charge. However, a congregation which doesn't read is missing one of God's greatest means for providing personal and spiritual growth.

15. Adequate space for a user-friendly foyer

Many churches have too many seats in the sanctuary and too little space in the foyer. Seldom is a church foyer too big. Churches need lots of space for people to mingle before and after church services. I know of a church that recently completed its new building with a foyer which doubles as a place for church dinners and banquets. It was the only way they could justify the space the people thought they needed for a really user-friendly foyer.

16. Religious background music

Foyer music that conjures memory, is easily recognized, and is piped in softly, may be a boon to some people but not necessarily to everyone. There is equipment available that will play a selected program, repeating itself multiple times. However, the churches I know who pipe music into their foyers do so primarily on week days to keep the church from seeming empty and dead.

17. Where are the drinking fountains?

Perhaps it is only a personal hang-up, but the availability of water fountains is a problem in scores of churches where I go to speak. When I ask an usher where the water fountain is, the way is almost always long and involved. Perhaps drinking fountains are not on the lists of church building committees when they consider the fine details in a building plan, or they are too far down the list to get full consideration. Also, I have often helped a struggling child up to a drinking fountain when he or she was not yet tall enough to drink from the adult fountain. For whatever it is worth, think about the need for a fountain that fits both children and adults. As a minimum, install a fountain somewhere in the main foyer with a second one in the hallway outside the choir room.

18. Restrooms and lounges

While personal facilities, including stations for changing diapers, are readily found in most churches, modest little signs that point the way to the restrooms are not. It is embarrassing to be forced to ask someone where the restroom is located although the need for such facilities is universal, and sometimes urgent. Make your restrooms modern, updated, clean, and available—and post a few signs so strangers may also know their location.

19. Special problems with multiple services

The need for greeters in churches with multiple services is complicated by the overlapping schedules. Holding back a foyer full of people while another congregation exits takes all the diplomacy a greeting ministry can muster. Also, it takes more than twice as many greeters to serve the foyer needs of churchgoers when there is an option of more than one service or Sunday school. Serving as greeters and parking lot people in a church with multiple services is an organizational challenge which needs to be faced in a meeting of the entire corps of greeters. Everybody's input is needed, and still the quality of the greeting ministry may suffer. Trying to do too much in too small a space does not add to the problems, it multiplies them.

20. A marquee or an umbrella

Bad weather calls for special skills among greeters. Greeters in churches without marquees—which is most churches— need a supply of large umbrellas to be used as car doors are opened in the rain or snow and families are assisted into the church. Each greeter needs to keep custody of his or her own umbrella and not pass it along to whoever needs it next. It is a personal piece of equipment for use in inclement weather so that greeters and parking lot workers can help protect worshipers from the elements.

21. Emergency procedures

Sooner or later, your church will have an emergency. Important telephone numbers need to be readily available at the information desk. Doctors, nurses, law officers, and other people usually needed in emergencies should be identified in advance. The most likely emergencies are heart attacks, seizures, accidents, children's problems, and persons given to disturbing the peace. Never panic. Be understanding. But act decisively according to a predetermined strategy.

22. Telephone and message service

Some people can attend services when they are on 24-hour call as long as they are promptly notified about incoming messages. This is reason enough for having a phone at the information desk. Others, though not on call, may also need word on incoming messages. Work out a plan for expediting these messages and make sure it is understood by all greeters and ushers.

23. Lost and found

If all the Bibles left in churches in one single year were stacked in a pile, the sight would be impressive. And a similar pile could be made of gloves and mittens in churches located in cold climates. Because churches are often reluctant to throw away anything people have left or lost, what to do with lost and found items can become a problem. To say the least, a single place needs to be identified for keeping lost articles with one person in charge. In addition, at least once each year an announcement should be made for people to identify Bibles and other lost belongings before they are given to a charitable agency. Nothing needs to be kept forever, not even a lost Bible.

24. Cards, pencils, and last week's bulletin

Some things people seldom call for are still important in the user-friendly foyer. When a rare need does arise it is satisfying to have the answer or the much-needed item available. That kind of service is equal to going the second mile. For instance, someone will surely need last week's bulletin, a copy of the tape of a sermon from last month, or the address of a missionary. A few plastic head coverings for ladies caught away from home in the rain are only needed when they are really needed. And pledge cards should always be available, even for writing messages to be left at the information desk. Your ingenuity and creativity must be counted on for supplying all the little things people occasionally need.

DISCUSSION QUESTIONS

1. What is your idea of a friendly foyer and how well does your church foyer measure up?
2. On an ascending scale from one to ten, how well do the bulletin boards serve the people in your church? What could improve them?
3. How well is your church progressing toward the ultimate strategy of a user-friendly church where everyone is a greeter?
4. What are the three "Cs" that relate to the effectiveness of your church foyer?
5. How effective are your information desk and sanctified book table operations?

4

A BETTER WAY
OF DOING THINGS

Once in a long span of years, someone comes along with a new idea whose time has come, or with an old idea which has been improved and repackaged for the next generation. Such was the late Sam Walton from Bentonville, Arkansas. Like Henry Ford, who transformed America's idea of transportation by providing the working man with an affordable automobile, Sam Walton transformed the shopping habits of ordinary people in small communities with his new discount stores on the edge of town. He did it with a three-point strategy: (1) quality merchandise for a reduced price; (2) oceans of convenient free parking; and (3) friendliness unlimited.

No one ever entered a Wal Mart without being faced by a smiling greeter with a down-home welcome. As he visited his stores, Sam Walton led his "associates" in the Sam Pledge: "From this day forward, every customer who comes within ten feet of me, regardless of what I am doing in this house, I am going to look him in the eye. I am going to smile. I am going to greet him with a 'Good morning,' or a 'Good afternoon,' or a 'What can I do for you?'—so help me Sam!"

After 28 years of commitment to good value, ample parking, and unlimited friendliness, it is no wonder that Sam Walton, when he died at 74 years of age, was the world's best known pick-up truck driver who owned 1,750 stores and who had surpassed Sears as the number one retailer in America. At least one-third of his formula focused on friendliness. And there must be a lesson there for all churches and church greeters.

Dwight L. Moody had the friendliness formula in his mind when he built the world's largest Sunday school in Chicago. He also had a three point formula: (1) cater to the street children and poor families other Chicago churches ignored; (2) teach children the gospel by teaching them to sing choruses and gospel songs; and (3) practice unlimited friendliness. Of course, he had greeters at his church doors. They were there as Moody's personal representatives, passing out love and friendship in the name and for the sake of Christ.

One cold January Sunday morning, when the frigid air came in off Lake Michigan with a fury only Chicagoans can understand, a shivering boy arrived late for Sunday school. He was ill-clad in an inadequate jacket held together at the neck with a safety pin. Short pants left his thin little legs unprotected against the unrelenting cold. His low-cut, hand-me-down shoes were no match for the deep snow. His legs were blue from the chill.

A church greeter picked up the small boy in his big, loving arms and began to massage his legs and arms to get the blood flowing faster. After a big hug, he stood the boy down at arm's length and said, "Where do you live, Sonny?"

When the boy told the church greeter his address, the man quickly calculated the youngster had walked nearly two miles one way in the bitter cold to attend Moody's Sunday school. "Why did you do it?" he asked. "You must have walked by a dozen church doors to come to Moody's Sunday school! Why did you do it?"

The boy's jaw went slack. He was a child with no ready answer. Then he looked up at the greeter and said carefully, "I guess it's 'cause they love a feller over here."

It is not possible to fake Moody's kind of love. Either you have a loving church or you don't. Moody once said he wished he could stand on the roof of his church and cry out to all of Chicago, "God loves you!" And somehow, when Moody said it, they believed him.

This chapter is dedicated to the better ways of doing things, by church greeters who are on the front line, saying what their whole church feels: "We love you, and we are glad you are here."

1. Make a spiritual commitment to the ministry of greeting

Paul provides greeters with the right perspective on their motivation for serving at the door of the church. "Whatever you do, work at it with all your heart, as working for the Lord, not for men, since you will know that you will receive an inheritance from the Lord as a reward. It is the Lord Christ you are serving" (Col. 3:23–24).

Learn to think kindness, and not to expect very much in return. Teens may barely look at you, never meeting your eyes with theirs. Mothers with children may be preoccupied with getting themselves and their brood into the church building without one of the youngsters falling or disappearing into the crowd. There may be reasons why a handshake is ignored by some people, or limply returned. But keep on being kind and friendly anyhow; you are serving the Lord. You are called to be faithful, not to be appreciated.

2. Concentrate on the people, one at a time

It is human to let everything someone says remind you of something about yourself, thus shifting the conversation from focusing on them to centering on you. This is a serious error in the etiquette of church greeters. Look people in the eyes. And above all, keep smiling and keep talking about them. In a 1961 speech, Adlai Stevenson said, "Flattery is all right if you don't inhale." No one will be upset because you say something nice about them in your greeting at the church door. But always talk about them, not yourself.

3. Concerning yourself

As I wrote in *The Usher's Manual*, "Conceit is repulsive, but self-assurance and self-respect are admired." Be sensitive to your own personal cleanliness and good grooming. Wear clothes that say "I care about how I look." Deodorant and mouthwash are the friends of greeters.

Be proud to be a greeter. Be affirming in things you say about your church and your pastor. There is no place for a judgmental attitude at the door of the church. Your face should be pleasant and your attitude prayerful. Make of yourself the kind of person you would like to meet if you were entering through your church door each Sunday.

4. Know your church

No one can know everything about his or her local church. But with a little effort it should not be hard to make a list of the questions asked most often. And when there is not an immediate answer, be ready to refer people to the right source, and then follow up to be sure their question was answered. There is no reason to be short on information about offices, telephones, restrooms, classrooms, exits, nursery facilities, literature, brochures, the church calendar, and last week's bulletin.

5. Remembering names

Some persons are more gifted than others in remembering names. However, the greeter who knows the most names is likely to be the most appreciated. Here are some suggestions:

- Listen to a name until you have accurately understood it, even if you need to ask for the name to be spelled out. Many people do not remember names because they do not listen, and therefore do not enter the name clearly into the computer of their mind.
- As much as possible, relate the name to something that is already easily remembered such as another person by the same name, or a well-known place. Most specialists in remembering names emphasize the importance of relating the name to some easily remembered person, place, or thing.
- Use the person's name at least three times as soon as possible. Start by calling the person by name even in the process of meeting him or her.
- Write down the name. One traveling minister who was famous for remembering many names in many places, always wrote down the name of a new acquaintance as soon as he was alone. He credited his immediate use of the name and his habit of writing it down as the most important factors in his ability to remember names.

6. Building an informal organization

The human tendency is to organize the church greeters too much or too little. In most churches, according to size, there is one person who is in charge of the team of greeters assisted by two captains who recruit and schedule the greeters on a rotating monthly basis. The job of the captain is to walk the hallways being sure every church entrance is well served. The job of the head greeter is to be sure everything runs smoothly, to preside over periodic meetings of all greeters, and to work with the captains on recruiting personnel. The ushers take over where the greeters leave off, by helping people to their seats.

In summary, keep the organization simple. Develop the system to fit the size and nature of your church. Every church needs a head greeter appointed by the pastor or the board. This assignment may be given to a couple or to one person. Whoever is appointed is in charge. He or she provides the necessary training, holds periodic meetings, gives general supervision to the greeting ministry, and is responsible for the operation of the user-friendly foyer.

The head greeter needs two associate head greeters. The job description for these captains may vary according to the size of the church. In small churches, their main responsibility is to recruit greeters and be sure they are in their places for each service. In larger churches, there may be a division of labor between the parking lot, the church foyer, and the secondary entrances. In still other churches, the greeters are recruited to serve alternate months, using more volunteers, and lowering the risk of overload or job weariness.

Regardless of the organizational pattern adopted, the basic rule is to keep it simple. It is much better to have too little organization and too little supervision than too much. It is possible to organize a ministry to death.

7. Dealing with disruptions

Things do happen which are not in the schedule. In these instances, the common sense of the greeter takes over while a quiet, dignified response is made that does not further disrupt things. The intrusion of social activists are a reality in our culture. Drugs abound. Alcohol sometimes goes to church.

Even mentally disturbed persons may gravitate toward the church, looking for acceptance or free expression. Whatever the cause of the disturbance, there is no place for panic among greeters and ushers. And the best insurance against panic is a predetermined strategy.

8. The importance of a few good policies and procedures

Since Paul has taught us that "the letter kills" and "the Spirit makes alive," no group of greeters needs a long list of negatives spelling out rules for greeters. However, policies on basic matters such as time of arrival, rotation of greeters and assignments, what to do when absences are required, and where to receive bulletins and other supplies, can actually further the work of the team. And remember, policies are most useful when they are written down.

9. Four biblical qualities of good greeters

Those who were appointed to serve tables in the Jerusalem church qualified by meeting four criteria: (1) a good reputation; (2) life in the Spirit; (3) wisdom; and (4) faith (Acts 6:1-7). Note: This passage is a good source for a greeter's devotional at the opening of a training session.

10. Four mundane qualities of a good church greeter

The person assigned to recruit greeters needs to keep several things in mind: (1) Include some married couples and some male and female singles in your cadre of greeters. It will surprise some people if a mature teenager is included in the roster of greeters. (2) People who make a good appearance enhance the witnesses for Christ and the church. (3) The twin virtues of a good church greeter are kindness and friendliness. (4) Personal hygiene deserves personal attention.

11. Proper introduction techniques

I know of a church with a policy that says that no greeter shall turn away from a new person or family in the parking lot, or in the foyer, until they have introduced them to someone else. One man told me he had been introduced nine times before he got into the church from the parking lot.

In this age of emphasis on equality, there are no old rules

of etiquette that call for the younger to be introduced to the older, or the person with less status to the person with more status. In the first century, when slaves and owners attended the same house-church, the Christian witness called for the equal importance of every person. James admonished the early church: "The brother in humble circumstances ought to take pride in his high position. But the one who is rich should take pride in his low position, because he will pass away like a wild flower" (James 1:9, 10). Introduce people with a clear enunciation of their name, and if possible, a few words about who they are and what identifying connections they may have in the community.

12. Three myths to forget

There is a myth which suggests that church greeters are not important, and may not be needed in smaller churches where everyone knows everyone else. The fact is that greeters are to the arriving worshiper what the teller is to the bank, or the waiter is to the restaurant. The money may be in the vault, the food prepared in the kitchen, and the sermon delivered from the pulpit, but the teller, the waiter, and the church greeter are visible first, working with the customers as they arrive for the service. And, to date, no one has projected any satisfactory replacements for those who work directly with people.

There is another myth which suggests anyone can be a greeter. However, it takes special skills to be an effective greeter just as it does to sing in the choir or teach in a classroom. Greeters drive the welcome wagon that connects the pastor with the arriving congregation. The front door experience of every arriving person or family is a high priority in user-friendly churches.

There is still another myth which suggests people don't care who is at the church door as long as it is open and they receive a bulletin. False. People enjoy seeing the same person, or the same couple, at the same door each week. Some people enter the same door each week just to be greeted by the person they expect to be there. And more than one pastor has gotten reports of people inquiring about the absence of a particular greeter on a given Sunday. People are creatures of habit who park in the same places, look for the same greeter at "our" door, sit in the same pew, and feel disappointed when a stranger is in the pulpit.

13. Four "don'ts" to remember

In the message on unconditional love in Paul's letter to the Corinthians, the apostle identifies four negatives which apply to all Christians, but especially to church greeters: Don't be (1) proud; (2) rude; (3) self-centered; or (4) easily angered (1 Cor. 13:4, 5). There is a reason for this discipline of the soul. "Do not forget to entertain strangers, for by so doing, some people have entertained angels without knowing it" (Heb. 13:2). Note: These seed thoughts may be used in the devotional moments at the beginning of a church greeters' meeting or training session.

14. The big dividends of follow-through

In 1854, Henry David Thoreau said in his book, *Walden*, "I have only received one or two letters that were worth the postage." And he further said, "We hate the kindness we understand." Thoreau hit an open nerve with all of us. We don't like phony friendliness or contrived kindness. When expressions of these virtues are affected instead of genuine, they tend to boomerang.

However, weekday follow-through by Sunday church greeters is disarming. An encouraging note, a friendly phone call, or arrangements for coffee together with a first-time visitor or an old-timer who is struggling with the stressful realities of a tough situation, may be your cup of cold water given in Christ's name.

15. A sense of the fitness of things

Finally, there is no way to cover all the possible situations greeters encounter. Underlying all the work done by this important unit of workers in every church is the plain matter of common sense, and the fact that effective greeting is more an attitude than it is a set of techniques. In his letter to the Galatians, Paul said, in effect, an attitude can never be set by law. ". . . kindness, goodness, faithfulness, gentleness, and self-control. Against such things there is no law" (Gal. 5:22, 23).

This means the church greeter's better way of doing things begins in the heart, cleansed by and filled with the love of Christ, and manifested in genuine expressions of kindness at the church door.

DISCUSSION QUESTIONS

1. Do you know friendly service people in local establishments whose story may be an encouragement to your greeters?
2. How is it possible for you as a greeter to concentrate on both the people and on yourself?
3. What are some suggestions for improving the ability to remember names?
4. What strategies can be developed for dealing with church-related disturbances and disruptions?
5. What are the four biblical qualifications for a good church greeter?

5

THE PARKING LOT MINISTRY

Although Americans have enjoyed a long-standing love affair with the automobile, cars have not always enjoyed good press. Winston Churchill said, "I have always considered the substitution of the internal combustion machine for the horse, marked a very gloomy milestone in the progress of mankind." When John Keats wrote his 1958 book on the American automobile, he called it *The Insolent Chariot*.

However, the role of the auto is fundamental in understanding the American scene and the attendance habits of churchgoers. The family car has required basic changes in the way Americans live. For instance, our houses are designed to take care of our cars. Cities are divided by freeways which have increased deterioration in some sections of town and stimulated growth and development in others. The one unquestioned symbol of the suburbs is not the tract house, but the automobile. The number of cars in the driveway usually indicates the number of adults living at home.

As congregations have moved to follow the housing preferences of their parishioners, or to escape the blight of their old neighborhoods on the wrong side of the freeway, they have been inevitably faced with tougher and tougher local regulations on adequate parking, including number of spaces, landscaping, lighting, and drainage.

However, since space for parking the family automobile has become an extension of many businesses, it is only natural that the parking lot is included in the responsibilities of church greeters in many churches. Churchill's longing for the simple ways of the horse are not widely shared. The car is here to stay, and its numbers on the road are increasing. In churches with multiple services, some families arrive in more than one car as they struggle to meet conflicting schedules.

The question is: How can we include the parking lot in the ministry of church greeters?

1. The red carpet treatment

One church I visited actually rolled out a red carpet from the front door of the church to the curb where helpful greeters opened car doors and helped families disembark. The carpet seemed to please everyone, especially the children. And it was a symbol of the importance the church and the greeters attached to the arrival of the congregation. Even without a red carpet, it is still possible to give people the feeling of a red carpet welcome as they roll up to the church in the family car.

2. Regulated parking

Regulated parking is a necessity in most church parking lots in cities. Small town and rural churches usually have parking spaces available for their parishioners in their own lot, on the street, and in the lots of adjacent businesses which are closed on Sundays. Very large churches with newer facilities have usually been forced by building codes to provide comfortable parking lots. Those churches with the biggest parking problems are often in places where all parking is at a premium because the church and all the other properties in the area were built before the updated parking codes were in place.

It may be unfair, but members arriving early are sometimes asked to park farthest from the church so more convenient spaces can be saved for others. Therefore, choir members, teachers, greeters, staff, and attendants who arrive early further serve their congregation by parking at a distance.

Except for persons using reserved spaces near the building, families need a warm-hearted greeter to assist in the parking process. It seems that fewer and fewer churches have the luxury of abundant parking which can be used haphazardly. Therefore, it takes attendants to make the best use of the space available. In all cases, an important priority is to train parking attendants to be church greeters and never let them reduce their assignment to directing traffic.

3. People with bundles

Many workers in the Sunday school arrive at church burdened down with packages and boxes that are cumbersome to handle. The availability of carts or wagons under the command of teenagers is a small but often-needed service to church workers.

4. The problems of multiple services

Two and three services on a Sunday morning can alleviate or complicate the challenge of parking for everyone. Properly marked lanes for entering and exiting the lot are mandatory. Ample time between services for clearing and refilling the parking lot is essential. And in almost every case, a multiple schedule requires kind-spirited, but efficient, men and women to supervise the process.

5. The use of multiple parking lots

Some of the large churches in old properties face the challenge of ample parking by using multiple lots on opposite sides of the church, sometimes across the street or around the corner. This parking pattern calls for a supervisor and cadre of greeters in each lot because separate areas must be operated on their own. If a crossing is involved, safety becomes a factor, and additional trained personnel are needed. Some churches use auxiliary business or school parking at considerable distances from the church. Those churches that have this arrangement request their own members to fill up the auxiliary parking areas first and therefore save the adjacent lots for new people and latecomers. In these situations, jitneys or vans are used to bring people from the farthest parking areas to the church door.

Each of these escalations in the complexity of the parking situation further confuses the matter and calls for more and better planning and supervision. In any case, protect the congregation from men with parking lot attendant mentalities who resort to ordering and monitoring. Make everyone in the parking lot a church greeter with all of the qualifications required of the church greeters at the foyer doors.

6. Valet parking

I have known of churches who provide valet parking for some people such as the infirm or elderly. However, this service opens up the possibility of church liability and therefore requires careful planning and monitoring plus ample liability insurance. Everyone's personality changes when his or her car is damaged.

7. The best use of the shuttle

Golf carts, vans, and specialty vehicles are of great service in some situations such as downhill parking. One church I visited used special vehicles that looked like old-fashioned street cars to bring people from the bottom of the hill where much of the church parking was located. The more unique the vehicle, the more people will adjust to the commuting process, especially the children. But regardless of the uniqueness of the vehicle, efficiency is the key to making a shuttle service work. A shuttle bus or train needs to be in sight the moment any family gets out of their car. Also, small station houses that are attractive and conveniently located may increase the popularity of a shuttle service.

8. One man's ministry

A wonderful layman, in a large church in Detroit, took on the parking lot of his church as a ministry. Because there were not enough parking spaces to meet the needs of the congregation at that time, he figured out a way to park the cars in a solid mass like the downtown commercial parking lots did. This meant he had to be on hand early with his carefully chosen and personally trained workers. The system worked because they figured a way to empty the lot without everyone leaving at the same moment. The procedure was effective although it took considerable attention both before and after church.

One Sunday, a motorist and his wife wheeled into the church parking lot intending to turn around. Before they could execute their turn, another car wheeled in behind them, and then, another, and another—and they were stuck.

The unsuspecting visitor explained to the parking attendant his intention to turn around. Now he was stuck and didn't know what to do. Rather than unravel the entire parking lot to let out this one car, the supervisor talked the man and his wife into staying for church. And they did. To everyone's surprise, they liked the service. They enjoyed the pastor, and they particularly enjoyed the congregational singing. On their way out, they even commented about the attitudes of the people. The person who saw his parking lot assignment as a ministry was thrilled. As the visitors drove away, he waved them a happy goodbye, never expecting to see them again. However, the next Sunday they were back on purpose. Other Sundays followed with the lay minister taking every opportunity before and after church to reinforce his growing friendship with the couple. Today, that once-upon-a-time-stranger who got into the parking lot by mistake is serving on the church board.

DISCUSSION QUESTIONS

1. How many parking spaces do you have for your church and how do the number of spaces fit the number of cars needed for your people on Sunday morning?
2. What specific things could you do to make your parking lot more beautiful as an extension of your sanctuary?
3. What services could you add in your parking lot that would enhance the Sunday morning experience of your congregation?
4. What is the current level of happiness with your parking facilities as they are, and what could you do to improve things without spending major amounts of dollars?
5. Do you have adequate supervision in your parking lot and workers who are greeters and not just traffic directors?